The People's History

The Gaunless Valley

by

Tom Hutchinson

This is captioned as West Auckland Colliery, but visual evidence suggests Randolph Colliery, Evenwood. Mr William is front row extreme right.

Previous page: A charabanc trip from Cockfield to High Force in the 1920s. Back right is Rufus Teasdale, the driver of the family firm's Fiat bus. The gentleman with the stick is Emmanuel Priestley. His wife next right.

Cover picture: Two young miners at a drift mine at Bolton Garths, Evenwood Gate about 80 years ago.

First published in 2001 by

The People's History Ltd
Suite 1, Byron House
Seaham Grange Business Park
Seaham, Co. Durham
SR7 0PY

ISBN 1 902527 73 9

Contents

Aerial photograph of High Lands in 1996. Opencast mining restoration behind the village. In the background is a line of trees identifying the course of the River Gaunless. Behind the river valley, on the right, is a straight line showing the course of the Bishop Auckland – Barnard Castle railway. The piers of Lands Viaduct may just be seen.

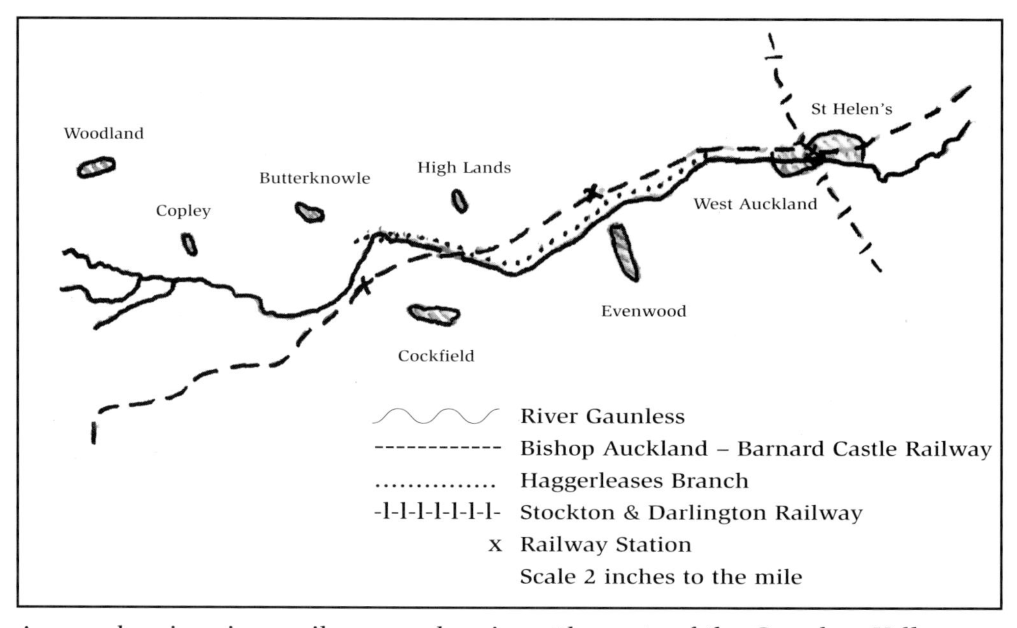

A map showing river, railways and main settlements of the Gaunless Valley.

Introduction

The River Gaunless is only about 14 miles long from Copley where its two main tributaries, Hindon Beck and Arn Gill meet, to where it joins the River Wear at Bishop Auckland. Within the area south west of West Auckland the Gaunless flows from the high fells of the Pennines through former mining villages and industrial remains towards more luscious pastures and arable land below Ramshaw. Apart from some opencast mining the area today is one of dormitory villages and white-washed farmhouses, pleasantly rural and quiet.

It is hard to think back at what the Gaunless Valley looked like in the heyday of collieries, cokeworks, quarries and railways in the hundred years or so from 1850. What remains today is only a fraction of what was visible on the ground, but the interested visitor can find much to explore in the Gaunless Valley, whether it is industrial remains or the landscape.

This book is an attempt to give the reader – whether local or a stranger – a photographic record of the people and places of the valley. Many of the illustrations are of old postcards and as the golden age of sending postcards was in the period from about 1900 to 1918, there are a number of views from that era when, co-incidentally, the Gaunless Valley was industrially at its height.

I have tried to give a comprehensive picture of the main settlements starting with Cockfield, then moving over the river to Woodland, Copley, Lands and Butterknowle, then back over to Evenwood, and finally to West Auckland and St Helen Auckland (usually called St Helen's) which are separated by the river. The final section covers mainly coal mining and railways which by their nature are dependent on each other. When mining disappeared, so did the railways.

The other main emphasis is on people – at leisure, at school, at work – over a hundred year period. People make places what they were and what they are today. The Gaunless Valley, at the southern limit of the Great Northern Coalfield, with its seams appearing at or near the surface would not have been developed, but for the ingenuity of man. This ingenuity was limited originally as the coal seams were faulted and thin, but the opening of the Stockton & Darlington Railway and what followed meant that waggonways and sidings could be easily built, and the river valley with large and small mines – a pit in every field it was said – became an economic powerhouse for over 100 years, and provided riches for the entrepreneurs and a livelihood for thousands of people.

I hope the pictures bring back fond memories of people and times past.

Tom Hutchinson
October 2001

View of Cockfield from the top of Gordon House pit headgear. In the foreground right is the parish church of St Mary and churchyard. Front Street, the main street, runs from right to left starting beyond the parish church. This postcard dates from about 1905-1910.

Acknowledgements

I would like to thank and acknowledge all contributors of pictures and information:

Beamish – The North of England Open Air Museum, The Gaunless Valley Local History Trust, Commission-Air, Bob Abley, Fred Alderson, John Askwith, David Barker, Ian S. Carr, Edwin Coates, Jim Coates, Tony Elliott, Sheila Harris, Derek Hewitson, Brian Hutchinson, Jim Jackson, Irene Kerr, Ray Law, George Nairn, Irene Parr, Colin & Winnie Priestley, Peter Redfearn, Gwen Sams, Colin Summerson, David Thom, George Thompson, Alan Thornton, Margaret Vickers, Jack Walker and Ken Walton. Special thanks to John Hallimond and Kevin Richardson for filling in the gaps and being generous with their time and knowledge.

Bibliography

Guide to the Gaunless Valley – Tony Hopkins/Don Wilcock
A Journey through the Gaunless Valley – The Gaunless History Trust
Banners of the Durham Coalfield – Norman Emery
Coal Mining in County Durham – Durham County Environmental Education Curriculum Study Group
Cockfield Matters – Ian Gomersall
Butterknowle in 1851 – Durham University
Evenwood and The Barony in 1851 – Durham University
Evenwood's Heyday 1896-1918 – Durham University
Old West Auckland and St Helen Auckland – Derek J. Hebden
Bishop Auckland Co-operative Society Jubilee History 1860-1910 – T. Readshaw
Stockton & Darlington Railway – P.J. Holmes
Memories of the LNER – South-west Durham – Allan W. Stobbs
Kelly's Trade Directories – 1906, 1925, 1938

COCKFIELD

The green. Children posed for the photographer. This postcard was posted in Cockfield by an E. Gargett and sent to Mr R. Gargett of Copeland Lane, West Auckland, and refers to calling at West tomorrow on the way to Bishop Auckland. The GPO was very efficient round about 1912-1918 when this card was sent.

Cockfield was first mentioned in 1188 when a local church was called Cockfield. In 1220 Robert de Cockfield, Lord of the Manor, became Sheriff of Yorkshire, and in 1243 John Vavasour married Alice, the daughter of Robert, and, in turn, became Lord of the Manor. At about the same time the land behind the present rectory was enclosed. Consequently, a farming village developed to the north of the present Front Street.

It was the Vavasours who first developed coal mining in Cockfield and there is a definite record of mining on Cockfield Fell in 1375. In 1410 Ralph Neville, Earl of Westmoreland and Lord of Raby purchased the Manor of Cockfield, but after a rebellion in 1569 the properties were forfeited to the Crown. In 1624 Sir Henry Vane bought the Manor of Cockfield, Raby Castle and Barnard Castle from the King for £18,000. The Vanes have been Lords of the Manor ever since.

Cockfield Fell is the largest Ancient Monument site in North East England. There is evidence here of Pre-Roman settlements as well as Medieval boundaries and field systems. The fell is of open access and grazed by horses and sheep; a system administered by the Fell Reeves. The coal seams here were just below the surface, with the Busty seam at 12-15 metres and the Brockwell another 20 metres below. This gave rise to bell pits and shallow diggings which are particularly common in the south west part of the fell.

Probably the most well-known name connected with Cockfield is Dixon. George Dixon (senior) was a coal owner, but it is two of his sons who achieved fame outside the village. George (junior) used coal for illuminating purposes, manufactured coal tar and pitch, and was also involved in mathematics, mineralogy, painting and engraving. His brother – Jeremiah – was a mathematician and surveyor, but it was in 1763 when Charles Mason and Jeremiah Dixon were sent to North America to define the boundaries between the provinces of Maryland and Pennsylvania – the well-known Mason-Dixon line in American folklore. They also surveyed the boundaries between Maryland and Delaware.

High End, Cockfield. People posing again. T.R. Finlay was the local postcard publisher who was in business in Cockfield mainly as a jeweller at the turn of the 20th century. This card was posted on 30th July 1908 to Newtown, Wales.

Ahead is Stirk's shop who are still in business today. Right of the shop is the 1899 chapel which was later used as a Sunday school and is now the village community centre. The tin chapel on the right disappeared a long time ago.

Front Street. In front of the King's Head public house. The policeman is possibly George Fryer who was the constable in the early 1900s. Albert Million was the publican at that time. The King's Head is still open today, but the square building next door is now a fish and chip shop.

Village view looking west; showing more of the road and trees than on the previous page. The road and paths are made up, so this postcard probably dates from the 1920s.

Greyhound Inn, on a postcard published over 90 years ago. William Brown was the publican licensed to retail spirits, wines, ale, porter and tobacco.

A northern tradition, the workingmen's club. In Kelly's Directory, 1906, Jasper Robson was manager and John Guy, secretary. The building itself was opened in 1907, though this postcard published by F.W. Wilson, Cockfield was not posted till 1922.

The war memorial was dedicated about 1933/4, and includes the names of 45 local men who died in the First World War and eight in the Second.

A group posed in front of George G. Chapman's grocers and confectioners shop in Cockfield. This postcard was from a friend in Cockfield to Miss F. Wilkinson, High Lynburn, Woodland sometime before or during the First World War.

The same shop as above, but in more inclement weather which would be familiar to many Cockfield residents.

St Mary's Parish Church was originally built towards the end of the 12th century, with major alterations taking place between 1865-67 to cater for a population increase from 647 to 1004 between 1851 and 1861. By 1901 the population had increased to 1833 so the church was extended by lengthening the nave westwards, and northwards by the addition of the north aisle in 1911 as seen on the left side of this postcard.

Methodism came to Cockfield at the end of the 18th century, and their first chapel was built in Draft Yard in 1854. The chapel on this card was erected in 1888 at a cost of £400 and is still thriving today.

Esperley Lane. It looks as though all the residents are outside posed for the photographer. Many of the men in the picture worked at Gordon House Colliery which was about 1/2 mile away across the field to the left. This postcard was sent from Mary to Private J.T. Buttle, No. 3 camp, DLI, Mortimer Road Schools, South Shields.

Burnt Houses. Raby Moor Inn on the left is still in business today. This card was sent on 14th August 1915 to Miss Mary Raine, 16 Baltic Street, Hartlepool. Both of these cards were published by F.W. Wilson, Front Street, Cockfield.

Cockfield FC, Wear Valley League Champions, 1907-08. Back left to right: J. Cowley, T.H. Walton, J.W. Walton, F. Walton, F. Forster. Third row: P. Rutherford, J.W. Bryan (treasurer) W. Everitt, J. Dickenson, F. Robson, E. Grey, W. Forster. Second row: R. Pinkney, J. Holliday, G. Linsley, J. Kirby (trainer). Front: S. Million, F. Hammond, H. Longstaff, W. Conlin, Jont Linsley.

Cockfield AFC who narrowly lost the Amateur Cup Final 3-2 to Leyton at Ayresome Park, Middlesbrough on 14th April 1928. The team was Raymond Wedge (back fourth left), George Dixon, George Coates, Walter Barker (back second left), Walter Harrison, Tommy Oldfield (back extreme right), Billy Longstaff, Andy Pearson, Billy Rutter (2 goals), Harry Thompson, Norman Kirby.

Cockfield School, 1940. Back, left to right: Eric Walker, Cecil Alderson, John Stevens, Colin Priestley, Ronnie Penberthy, Fred Hammond, Jim Coates, ? Dowson, Eric Hammond. Middle: Doris Coates, Irene Appleby, Mina Heckley, Mabel Corner, Jenny Wake, Mavis Findley, Renie Tanner, Sylvia Race, Mary Hodgson. Front: Derek Wood, Joyce Lamb, Beryl Sams, Jean Buttle, Mary Wilkinson, Lilian Raine, Elsie Stephenson.

Cockfield School, 1949. Back, left to right: Brian Wallace, Russell Corner, Barry Bowes, Melvin Clark, John Chapman, John Shipton, David Bowman, Gavin Pearson, Miss Pattison. Third row: Neville Chapman, David Barker, Ann Everitt, Deirdre Makepeace, Nancy Wilkinson, Sheila Hogg, Margery Davison, John Finlay, Kenneth Hallimond. Second row: Sheila Armstrong, Judith Hammond, Celia Vickers, Margaret Blackett, Ann Allen, Gwen Hodgson, Sylvia Pears. Front: Melvin Waldock, Brian Sams, David Alderson, George Fee, Dennis Marquis, Jim Wilson.

Cockfield Boys Club, 1937. Back, left to right: Edgar Brittan, Alf Appleby, John Lowson, Maurice Rand, unknown, Vernon Linsley, Ronnie Heaviside, Chas Deighton. Front: Wilf Pinkney, Zeich Hope, George Daniels, Cyril Gargett, John Suckling.

Cockfield Village Outing to the Lake District in Jack Hall's coach, about 1952. The party included: Colin & Winnie Priestley, Margaret Dent, Grace & John Haddon, Jack & Emma Woodruff, Mrs Linsley, Jack Hall, Dora Nodding, Elsie Aulton, Ethel Watson, Phyliss Walton, Mrs Kathleen McDonald, Roy & Violet Linsley, Glynis Walton, Annie Pears, Leslie & Doreen Race, Miss Kathleen McDonald, Elizabeth, Ronnie, Patricia & Joan Pedelty, Emily Race, George Haddon.

Two pictures of Cockfield Methodist Male Voice Choir – the founding members in 1947 and members in the 50th Jubilee year, 1997.
1947 – left to right: Willie Forrest, Steve Wood, Alf Gargett, Percy Kirby, Jack Hodgson, Victor Sewell, Edwin Coates, Kit Wood, David Appleby, Albert Kirby, John Rand, Wilf Everitt, Jack Coates.
1997 – left to right: Edwin Coates, Joe Harding, Colin Priestley, David Thompson, Terry Gilder, Kenneth Robson, Bob Parr (front), Ray Horner (back), Cyril Wallace, Peter Metcalfe, Arnold Smith, Michael Henderson, Nigel Watson, Tony Mawer.

Road Gang in Cockfield in about 1933/34. On the extreme left is William Place and on the far right next to the horse, Walter Stevens.

Miners at Gordon House Colliery in the early 1920s. Back left to right: Wilf Gray, Wilf Hall, Dave Morley, Alf Simpson, Bert Chapman. Front: Judd Dowson. Note the 'midgy' lamps.

Two contrasting sporting pursuits. Jack Holliday (nickname Waugh Holliday who had a kick like a mule) from Cockfield who played league football for Brentford & Middlesbrough, and Matt Walton with his pigeon trophies in 1961.

BUTTERKNOWLE, COPLEY, LANDS & WOODLAND

Woodland. The Edge Hotel is behind the motor vehicle. Cuthbert Dowson was the publican in 1906. On the right is Thompson's shop and beyond the Butterknowle Coal Co offices.

The area north of the Gaunless has no settlement the size of Cockfield. Woodland lies at 1100 feet on top of the ridge that separates the Wear Valley from its major tributary, the Gaunless. The village is on the extreme edge of the Durham coalfield, but the seams are very near the surface. So much so that a local garage had its petrol pumps embedded in a seam and the foundations of two new bungalows have also been dug into one.

Butterknowle gives its name to the celebrated geological fault which greatly influenced mining in the locality. Enormous movements of the land resulted in horizontal rock strata being displaced resulting in a 'down throw' of between 240 and 600 feet. To miners this meant that a rich coal seam could end abruptly and re-appear a great distance from the original seam. Butterknowle and its smaller neighbours Copley, South Side, Lands and Wham were originally settlements of scattered farms and dwellings. However, the coal seams had been exploited since the 14th century and by the beginning of the 19th century Butterknowle was the largest township in Hamsterley Parish which extended as far north as the River Wear. From about 1830 industrial development saw village cores in these Gaunless villages, with a parish church being opened at Lynesack in 1848 and an adjacent school following four years later.

Two personalities played a part in the industrial development north of the Gaunless. Firstly, the leasee of the largest coal royalty, the Revd William Luke Prattman, ensured that the Stockton & Darlington Railway built its Haggerleases Branch by threatening to oppose the railway bill in the House of Lords. Ironically he eventually went bankrupt in 1841 and his Diamond Pit at Butterknowle was put up for auction. The second personality was John Hardy of Edge House, Woodland who leased Crake Scar Colliery and generally took 'pride in promoting the prosperity of Lynesack and Softley'.

Woodland. St Mary's Church was one of the many corrugated iron buildings erected in Woodland about 100 years ago, and is still in use today. Not so the old school building to the left. This postcard was sent by Herbert at Meadow View, Woodland on 6th October 1920. He says the (war) memorial at the front of the cemetery was unveiled on Saturday, but he was not there because he had the measles!

A long view of Woodland, along Middleton Road towards the south-west in 1930. This card was sent from Derby to Mrs J. McCartney, Milestone House, Woodland on 4th August 1930 from her daughter Florrie who was working in Derby.

Inclement weather in Woodland in 1965. A sudden snowstorm leaves its mark at Milestone Cottage. This cottage is the one shown middle right in the previous view.

Copley. A view along the main road towards Woodland. The shop on the left is still there, but empty and derelict. I wonder how long the children had to hold this pose 85/90 years ago?

Copley Lead Mill. This lead mill was the only one in the area and thrived in the 18th century, though by 1890 it was derelict. Ore was brought in by donkeys who carried coal on the return journey to Egglestone. The manager's house on extreme right, the cottage nearest the bridge over the Gaunless, and the house left middle distance are still lived in today. The rest of the buildings including the furnace have gone.

A general view of Haggerleases including the railway goods yard. Behind the trucks is Haggerleases Mill and the adjacent Mill House. Many of those buildings are no longer there today.

Bridge at the western end of the Haggerleases Branch of the Stockton & Darlington Railway, completed in 1830. Both the above views indicate how the branch railway closely followed the river bed of the Gaunless.

Floods occurred in the Gaunless Valley in 2000. The most serious were at South Church and West Auckland in June, but there was flooding further up the valley in November – as here at The Slack in the top picture and backing up the road towards Butterknowle in the lower picture.

This is the main street of High Lands in 1950 when mains electricity was being installed in the village.

This scene of 'leisure' interests of boxing and whippet racing is in front of the Black Swan Inn, High Wham. George Sewell was the publican at the time which suggests the view is from about 100 years ago. He was identified as the publican in Kelly's 1906 Directory. The inn was later converted into cottages.

Diamond Terrace, Butterknowle. Stone Row to the right. These houses overlooked the pit of the same name. G. Wilkinson of Butterknowle published this postcard and the others on this double page. The card was sent to a Master Ernest Dixon, Front Street, Sacriston from his Mother telling him that she had arrived safely, and was going on to West Auckland.

A horse and cart in Pinfold Lane, Butterknowle. The newsagents on the extreme right has an enamel plate advertising the 'Northern Echo'.

West View, Butterknowle. The local Co-op is on the extreme right in the distance. Modern housing now covers the Co-op site. This card was also sent to Draper House, Front Street, Sacriston, but to Mrs Dixon on 23rd June 1915 from her sister Rose. What is interesting is that this card is owned by a gentleman who lives in Cockfield, whilst the one on top of page 28 was bought by the author.

The Slack, Butterknowle, with the bridge over the Gaunless. Chimney of Diamond Colliery top left. The colliery was opened in 1835 by local entrepreneur, William Pratman. It was a small pit, typical of many in the Gaunless Valley, and only employed 18 men in 1896.

Lynesack Church. The Church of St John, the Evangelist, was erected in 1848 and renovated in 1892. In the churchyard is the grave of Edward Smith who died in 1884, and is identified as the character 'Smike' in Charles Dickens 'Nicholas Nickleby'. At the front right of the view is the infants school opened in 1852. It is now a private dwelling.

Lynesack Infants School, 1922. Back: Kenny Wilkinson, Willie Coates, Stanley Stubbs, Fred Alderson, Vincent Mudd, Willie Brownbridge, Stanley Collinson, Stanley Allinson, Johnny Dent, Jimmy Brunskill. Middle: Adeline Lee, ? Morton, Laura Wilson, Verna Waters, Nellie Anderson, unknown, unknown, unknown, ? Morton. Front: Bobby & John Alderson, Clifford Gargett, Laurence Coates, Lorna Foster, Sally Stubbs, Edna Richardson, Grace Gill, Violet Nelson, Dennis & Lionel Bell. At that time Thomas Clough was the headmaster.

Woodland Pit Banner Group, Durham Miners Gala, 1924. Mr Teasdale was bandmaster. The group included: Owen Doyle, Herbert Morton, Bob Wade, Joe Minto (trombonist), Jack Teasdale, Bob & Bert Moore, Jack Alderson (double bass), Tot & Frank Waller, Rupert Blackett, Bill Teasdale, Bob Appleby, Jack Waller, Fearon Brown, Joe Race, Ernest Moore. This pit was opened in 1837 by Sharp and Hardy. By 1867 the Woodland Collieries Co Ltd were working the Five Quarter and Main seams. Later that company went into liquidation and the pit was taken over by Cargo Fleet Iron Co. The pit closed around 1926. Woodland, employing 176 men in 1896, and Crake Scar Colliery were connected to the North Eastern Railway at Lands by a $4^{1}/_{4}$ mile branch line.

Woodland and Crake Scar Collieries Officials, August, 1913. Back left to right: John Walton, overman & master borer, J.W. Campbell, surveyor, Jas Hardy, cokeburner & heapkeeper, R.T. Waller, assistant engineer, W. Wilson, back overman, A. Johnson, back overman, J. Paterick, weighman, R. Shaw, overman, Alf Beadle, clerk. Front: Chas Johnson, bankmanager, E. Pattinson, cokeburner & heapkeeper, John Waller, engineer, J.J.C. Allison, agent & manager, Owen Hardy, head clerk, John Wallace, undermanager, Luke Timmins, storekeeper & weighman, Hutton Hall, undermanager.

Violet Orchestra, late 1930s. From left: Tom Sowerby, Copley, John Liddle, Cockfield, Fred Alderson, Woodland, Jacky Kirby, Esperley, Wilf Hammond, Cockfield, Percy Bradley, Cockfield.

Swimmers at Flaggy Dam, above The Slack. Not a scene which you would easily find today!

Butterknowle FC, Winners of Gaunless Valley League, 1910-11. Back, left to right: P. Simpson, E. Walton, unknown, A. Priestley, T.W. Kipling, G. Wilson, J. Race, J. Bates, T. Simpson. Middle: A. Thompson, J. Lamb, J.H. Sowerby. Front: J. Liddle, J. Mackay, N. Vickers, F. Dalkin, W. Neasham. Children not identified.

Lands FC, 1918. Back left to right: Joe Craggs, Will Morley, unknown, unknown, Fred Wardle, unknown, Fred Adams. Middle: Jack Hewitson, unknown, unknown, unknown, unknown. Front: Jonna Simpson, unknown, Tommy Oldfield, Matt Arnison, unknown, unknown.

The enthusiasm of youth at the sports day at Butterknowle School, 1933. Tipping the bucket!

Lands CC, Cup Winners, 1914. Cricket has always been very popular in High and Low Lands.

Lands CC, 1933. Back left to right: Ernie Liddle, Jim Roe, Will Chapman, Billy Dowson, George Oldfield, Jack Denham, Norman Watson, Henry Stainthorpe, Billy Linsley, Verdun Watson, Ernie Heslop. Middle: Mark Lee, Wilf Watson, G. Armstrong, C. Ferry, Bert Chapman, Billy Denham, Gilbert Denham. Front: John Metcalf, Ronald Clark, Herbert Wardle, Thomas Emerson Morley.

Lands CC, 1978. Mid Durham League Winners. Back left to right: John Little, John Tallentire, Peter Watson, Brian Longstaffe, Leonard Blackburn, John Long. Front row: Maxwell Oldfield, Robert Tookey, Neville Thompson, Robert Little, Colin Elliott.

Lands Women's Institute, 1961. Back row, left to right: Doris Hutchinson, Ena Parr, Elsie Hillary, Florence Lowson, Mattie Dowson, Freda Bainbridge, Dorothy Stainthorpe. Middle: Catherine Handley, Agnes Kellett, Mary Wardle, Alice Hutchinson, Rhoda Stephenson, Mrs Oliver, Mabel Linsley, Edna Denham, Mary Clarke. Front: Bessie Clark, Keziah Denham, Lizzie Bainbridge, Carrie Medd, Jane Ann Simpson, Edith Hewitson.

Lands Sunday School, 1975. Back row, left to right: Andrew Walker, Darren Marriott, Alison Danby, Maxine Oldfield, Julie Barker, Marie Walker. Middle: Paula Dowson, David Armstrong, Mark Carraway, Paul Elliott, Pamela Elliott, Amanda Elliott, Dean Marriott. Front: Amanda Carr, Richard Elliott, Joanne Elliott, Deborah Marriott, Philip Elliott, Michele Oldfield. The Wesleyan Chapel was opened in 1876, so this photograph is from the centenary year.

EVENWOOD

Evenwood. View from Railey Fell across the railway towards the Oaks part of the village. The Oaks were colliery houses built in the 1850s, with 2/3 small rooms and earth closets opposite their front doors. They were demolished in the 1950s. This postcard was published by Wilson's of Cockfield.

Evenwood is situated on the top of a steep hill on the south bank of the Gaunless. In ancient times it was one of the places given by King Canute to the church of Durham. At the end of the 13th century a great hunting park was formed here by the Bishop of Durham. Industry was first recorded in 1368 when Bishop Hatfield granted a lease for an iron furnace in Gordon and Evenwood Park at a rent of 16 shillings (80p) per week. In 1388 a coal mine was leased to John de Merley and others for £22 per annum, and in 1646 a large colliery called Thorne was leased to a Mr Drake at £70 per year, and re-let by him to Charles Vane and Thomas Bowes for £350.

Evenwood was typical of many other places in South West Durham in that coal mining could not compete with that of navigable parts of the rivers Tyne and Wear until the costs of transportation could be drastically reduced. This occurred with the coming of the railways, beginning with the opening of the Stockton & Darlington Railway in 1825.

The result was that the population of Evenwood and Ramshaw increased from 785 in 1821 to 1729 in 1841, 2674 in 1861 and 3882 in 1891. Major collieries at Randolph, Railey Fell, Norwood and Storey Lodge employed a total of 1037 men in 1896. A population peak of 5109 was reached in 1921, but by that time coal production in County Durham had passes its height and Evenwood's population dropped in every decade until 1951 when it was 3090. It seems to have generally stabilised nowadays, to 2749 in 1991.

Shirley Terrace about 1910. Walter Willson's shop on the left. Next to it was the draper's shop of Howson & Ray of Barnard Castle. Eventually Walter Willson's expanded and took over the next door shop when owned by a Mrs Brennan and Mrs Stonebank. The combined shop is still there, but closed as at August 2001.

The village on a postcard sent in April 1916 from Hilda at Evenwood to Miss Errington at 195 Talbot Road, Tyne Dock. The Randolph Institute in the middle was built in 1898 by the North Bitchburn Coal Co in commemoration of Queen Victoria's Diamond Jubilee the previous year. It is now a doctor's surgery. Another Wilson's of Cockfield published postcard.

Ramshaw, with the bridge over the Gaunless in front, the Haggerleases branch of the (after 1863) North Eastern Railway (NER) behind, and further back the Bishop Auckland – Barnard Castle branch of the NER. Evenwood station was in Ramshaw, to the left of the postcard view on the Barnard Castle line. At the middle left over the river is the site of Norwood Colliery, opened 1830s, closed 1904, then limited opening again until 1937. Just below the skyline in the middle distance was West Tees/Railey Fell Colliery which was open from 1863 to 1939. Both collieries employed a total of 428 men in 1896.

Two postcards from Evenwood showing the main street in about 1960. T.S. Anderson had already been in business for 50 years at this date as they appear in Kelly's Directory, 1906. Today, the shop is still there, but closed up. The school on the right of the lower card is Evenwood C. of E. School which had originally opened in 1865 and enlarged three times around the turn of the last century. It is now a community centre.

Evenwood Parish Church was built in 1867 at a cost of £2,780. It was restored in 1890/1 and could then seat 320. There was a fire at the church on 29th December 1907. Other than the shell, the church inside, along with the roof, was almost completely destroyed. The bottom postcard was photographed from inside the church looking towards the altar. The top postcard sent on 22nd April 1916 shows it in its rebuilt form after re-opening in March 1909 by the Bishop of Durham, Handley Moule.

Primitive Methodist Church, Evenwood. This church was built in 1912. The Primitive Methodists were long established in the village, with a tradition dating back to before 1840 when the preachers and their congregation were the backbone of unionism in the pits. This building is now a church hall.

A postcard showing the stationmaster and two ladies on the platform at Evenwood in North Eastern Railway days. Is this George H. Coates who was the stationmaster in 1906?

A group at the bottom of Victoria Street in 1947/8. From left to right: Gwen Proud, Mary Elizabeth Proud, Freda Proud, Mrs Woolard, Alice Young, Minnie Welsh.

A Golden Wedding Anniversary in 1959. Arthur and Anne Bennett with their six daughters, from left Lesley, Elsie, Avril, Millie, Hilda and Edna. They are sitting outside Ramshaw Chapel.

The unveiling of Randolph Colliery new (2nd) pit banner in May 1954. In front of the banner left to right: Eddie Banks, Lodge Secretary and checkweighman, Hugh Dalton, MP for Bishop Auckland, Jack Bell, retired checkweighman, Lodge Official and local councillor, and Harry Clarkson, Lodge Chairman.

Randolph Colliery. Hutton Drift miners in 1961, the year before the drift mine shut. Back left to right: Ronnie Lamb, Jim Clark, Jackie Bell, Jack Towers, Norman Robson, C. Patterson. Front: Freddy Bell, George Knight, Alf Sams.

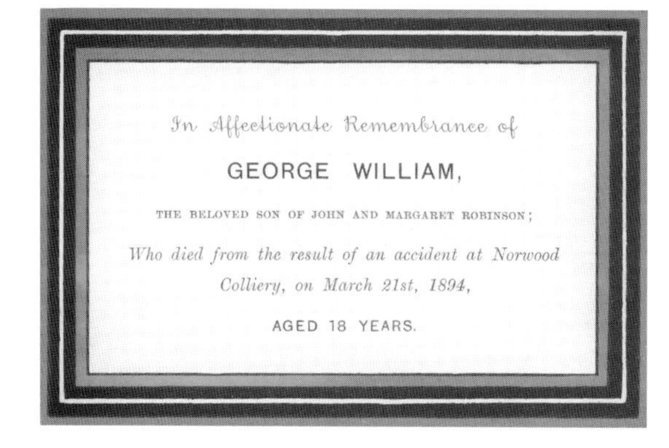

In Affectionate Remembrance of

GEORGE WILLIAM,

THE BELOVED SON OF JOHN AND MARGARET ROBINSON;

Who died from the result of an accident at Norwood Colliery, on March 21st, 1894,

AGED 18 YEARS.

A reminder of the dangers and tragedies of coal mining. An 'In Memorian' card in affectionate remembrance of George William Robinson who died from the result of an accident at Norwood Colliery on 21st March 1894 – aged 18 years.

The Scout movement in different eras. The top group is from about 1900 in Evenwood. The bottom group of Wolf Cubs dates from approx 1960. They were the District Totem Winners and included: Back left to right: Bryan Tate, Assistant Cub Master, Dennis Hewitt, Cub Master, Ray Law, Assistant Cub Master. Third row: Bobby Black, Allan Nicholson, Leonard Gallagher, George Atkinson, Kevin Maughan, Graeme Hammond. Second row: Jim Atkinson, Tim Hicks, Peter Bailey, Michael Clennell, Barry Redfearn, Peter Hull. Front: Paul Trotter, Ralph Fuller, David Watson, Malcolm Parkin, Arnold Bradwell, Colin Birch.

These pictures depict people when times weren't so good.

The Soup Kitchen Staff at Evenwood posed on 4th July 1921.

The Home Guard of 1941/2 set up to protect Evenwood in the Second World War.

Evenwood Juniors, 1921-22. Winners Auckland Junior League and Cup, Durham Junior Challenge Cup, Eden Hospital Cup, SW Durham Divisional Cup, County Medal Competition. Played 27, won 25, drawn 2. Goals for 83, against 17. Players names only, back three, left to right: Redfearn, Purdy, Snowball. Middle three: Mason, Lowson, Butterfield. Front six: Harrison, Stones, Clennell, Hooper, Metcalfe, Bowman. Mascot: F. Simpson. Inset left: J. Kirby, right: Dr A. Campbell, President.

Evenwood School Team, approx 1950-1. Back row, left to right: Jackie Clinton, Donald Ridley, Ronnie Tate, David Penman, Colin Blackett, John Barlett. Front: Brian Williamson, Bobbie Tate, Brian Purdy, Jackie Bell, John Bowman.

Fire at Evenwood Football and Cricket Clubs. On 6th September 1953 the wooden dressing rooms, pavilion and equipment were destroyed in a fire, causing damage in the region of £3000. The new building costing £4500 was completed a year later. In the meantime the tiny cricket score box was used as a referees changing room!

Evenwood Town FC, 1936, winners of the Northern League Challenge Cup by defeating Trimdon Grange 3-2 at Kingsway, Bishop Auckland. The Evenwood scorers were George Emmerson (penalty), Tommy Scott and Bill Singleton. In the picture is back 6th left, Walter Mairs, 7th left Percy Newton (goalkeeper) and 10th left Mr Blaiklock, the local pit manager. Third left front, George McCutcheon, vice-captain. Other players were: Tommy Wood, Wilf Buttle, John R. Firman and Ray Hunter.

Evenwood Town, 1948-49. Their first Northern League Championship season. Back left to right: Wilson, Walton (trainer), Cliff Lancaster, Johnny Wharton, Stan Blakeburn, George Wilson, Bobby Webb, Watson, Bobby Hanson, Ken Humble, Graham. Front: Joe Richardson, McDonald, Wilson Carr, Stan Peacock (captain), Allan Hogg, Jackie Kilcran, George Heaviside (Secretary). A record home crowd saw them clinch the championship by one point from Bishop Auckland by beating Crook Town 2-0 with goals from Joe Richardson and Wilson Carr.

Evenwood Town, 1969-70. Winners of the Northern League, 1969-70, 1970-71. Winners Durham Challenge Cup, 1969-70, runners-up, 1970-71. Back, left to right: Tommy O'Connor, Phil McNulty, Bob Tookey, John Noddings, John Hussey, Colin Hallimond, Tony Monkhouse, John Suddes, Bobby Black. Front: Derek Newton, John Weir, Eddie Ross, Ray Young, Brian Newton, Stuart Leeming, Brian Cunningham.

Evenwood Cricket Club, 1956 – the year before they temporarily disbanded! Back left: Bert Nicholson, Cyril Nicholson, unknown, unknown, Arthur Oldfield, Billy Clennell, Jossy Jackson. Front: Alan Welch, John Heaviside, Norman Bolton, Jack Kilcran, Cliff Mathews, George Daniels.

Evenwood Cricket Club, 1966. The club re-formed and in this year won the Mid-Durham Senior League Division Three Trophy and were finalists in the W.S. Franklin Cup losing after a replay to Crookhall! An unusual happening in cricket – the scores were tied on 101 in the first match. Back left: R. Proud, R. Hull, R. Tate, B. Longstaff, L. Sams, R. Jacobs, Front: J. Wearmouth, D. Jacobs, M. Parkin, A. Welsh, A. Teasdale, A. Thompson, E. Proud.

West Auckland & St Helen Auckland

West Auckland – The Green. The road bearing to the left is to Staindrop and Barnard Castle; to the right partly hidden by the trees is the A68 road to Corbridge. The public house in the middle is the Eden Arms. This postcard was sent from West Auckland on 10th August 1915 and up-dated Miss M. and J.A. Gowland of 18 Alma Terrace, Folly, Ryton-on-Tyne of the happenings over a few days, from J.E.A. Johnson. The card publishers, A. Ramsden & Son, produced a number of cards of West Auckland, and are thought to be travelling photographers.

In a 'History of the County Palatine of Durham' published in 1860, West Auckland is described as 'a considerable village on the road to Staindrop and Barnard Castle where it is crossed by that from Darlington to Wolsingham. Several of the houses bear traces of antiquity. The labouring population are for the most part engaged in works connected with colliery undertakings.'

St Helen Auckland is similarly described as 'situated three miles S.S.W. of Bishop Auckland on the road from that place to Barnard Castle, and contains several public houses, shops and tradesmen.'

However, both places are of ancient origin in that West Auckland is mentioned in 1183 in the Boldon Book, and the church of St Helen is a stone building dating from the 11th and 12th centuries. By 1860 though, both villages were very much industrially orientated with collieries at St Helen's, West Auckland and Norlees. In 1896 the two main collieries at St Helen's and West Auckland employed 920 men – about 20% of the total population, and were to be the mainstay of the economies of both places well into the last century. Unfortunately, as with other places in South West Durham, the Depression of the 1930s put many men out of work, and the unemployment rate in the Bishop Auckland area in 1932 was 60%. Mining continued after the Second World War, but by 1967 all mines in the Gaunless Valley had gone.

In the last 30 years new council housing and private estates have replaced the old 19th century properties in the two villages. Many of the most important architectural and historical buildings have been preserved. Unfortunately, traffic, particularly in West Auckland, is as heavy as ever.

Old Manor House, West Auckland. The manor house is now a hotel and country club, but in former days was the focal point of a large country estate dating originally from the 13th and 14th centuries; though the present building dates from the 17th and 18th centuries. It was once owned by the Eden family. The publisher of this card was G. Ramsay, Stationer, Post Office, West Auckland – he was in Kelly's Directories in 1925 and 1938.

The north side of The Green at West Auckland in the late 1920s. Note the child peering at the photographer from the pram. In front of the pram is the A68 road off to Corbridge to the left. A card sent on 12th September 1928 from Florrie to Mr and Mrs Stonehouse, 17-18 Plessey View, Blyth. The card publisher, G. Prudhoe & Co, Darlington, produced at least seven cards in this West Auckland series.

Front Street, West Auckland on the north side of the Village Green. On the left is the Rose & Crown public house. At about the time of this card's publication, say 90 years ago, the landlord was John Hughes. It is now a private house. Next door is the house where Mary Ann Cotton lived immediately before being arrested for the murder of three sons/stepsons and her lover. The inquest on her stepson, Charles Edward, was held at the Rose & Crown.

Old Church and Vicarage, St Helen's. The church dates from 11th and 12th centuries, though has been restored many times in the last 900 or so years. Originally the road went behind the church, and the stream in front has disappeared.

Interior, St Helen's Church. In the church is a stained glass window memorial to William Byers Kilburn, a well-known local surgeon who performed the autopsies on four 'victims' of Mary Ann Cotton.

West Auckland Cemetery opened in 1894 and situated in Darlington Road. Prior to that burials took place at St Helen's.

Maude Terrace, St Helen's. This is on the main road from Bishop Auckland to Barnard Castle, and the houses are typical of those erected in the late 19th century to house the industrial working class. The last four views come from postcards published by Geo. Chamberlain whose family was in business as grocers principally in St Helen's at the turn of the 19th century at least until 1925.

Church View, St Helen's. This card was posted in Bishop Auckland in 1921 from Percy and sent to Mrs Kirby, 12 Dene Bridge, Chilton.

Front Street, St Helen's. This and the previous view are basically part of the same road now called Manor Road, St Helen's. This card is of the style of Geo. Chamberlain, though the publisher is unnamed.

West Auckland Wesleyan Church. Erected in 1893 at a cost of £1550 and 'opened' by Sir Joseph Pease. It is still in use today, in contrast to the Primitive Methodist Church, diagonally opposite which is now a pine centre.

New Schools, St Helen's. New in 1846 and rebuilt in 1883. This postcard, publisher C. Smithson, Shildon, was posted at Bishop Auckland on 24th August 1909 and refers to horse racing at Redcar.

West Auckland – a view along the north side of The Green with the Queen's Head, selling Lorimer's Edinburgh Ales, in the middle of the picture. This photograph was taken in about 1930. John Kay was the licensee at about that time.

Greyhound Inn, West Auckland on the corner of The Green and Darlington Road. The landlord, Tom Sowerby, and three of his customers are posing for the camera. This postcard dates from approx 1910. On the site now is a modern bungalow.

Village Pont, West Auckland. The drinking water supply came for over 40 years from this pont, which was supplied with water from a reservoir at the west end of the village. Eventually, when Waskerley reservoir was opened in 1872, the pont fell into disuse. However, the pont is still there today, but now described as the Jubilee Monument (Queen Victoria's) with an appropriate dedication on a stone plaque.

Derelict Watermill at West Auckland. This photograph was taken in the last 30 years, but there is evidence of a watermill at West Auckland in 1647 when it was leased by a William Gargrave.

Sydney Pickles' Monoplane at West Auckland just before the First World War. Mr Pickles was from the Saltburn area and his plane is a 2-seater designed by Robert Blackburn. Presumably he was out for a spin and landed at West?

The Women's Institute, West Auckland in the 1950s. Mrs Jenny Williams second row from front, second right.

The next four cards are from the family album of the Thom family. David Smart Thom joined the police at Bishop Auckland in 1874, moved to West Auckland in 1887, and became landlord of the Talbot Hotel, West Auckland from 1903 to 1913.

Daisy Thom and Walter King's Wedding on 23rd March 1904. Standing left to right: George Ricardo William Thom (brother), John King (groom's father), Walter King, David Smart Thom (father), Lily Tate (sister). Seated: June Ann Hope (?), Daisy Thom, Catherine Thom (mother). Front: William McClymont Thom (brother), Catherine Thom (sister), unknown, Daisy McGregor Tate (niece), Chrissie Banks Thom (sister).

The Thom Family, 1913. This photograph was possibly taken in the yard of the Talbot Hotel where David Smart Thom was the landlord following his retirement as a sergeant from the police. The picture shows David, wife Catherine and their sons and daughters. Standing left: Chrissie Banks, William McClymont, Lily, Robert McCombie, Daisy, George Ricardo William. Front: David Smart (son), David Smart (father), Catherine (daughter), Catherine (mother), Charles Davidson.

West Auckland Cycling Club, about 1908. Back, second left: William McClymont Thom. Third row, third left, Joe Tate (son-in-law), 6th left, David Smart Thom. Front row, left: George Ricardo William Thom.

Locomotive Inn, St Helen's, about 1912. Charles Davidson Thom posing in the front doorway. He was landlord from approx 1906-1914. Nowadays the inn is closed and boarded up.

West Auckland Durham Miners' Association Banner with the lodge members. This banner, dating from around the First World War, shows standing William House who became in 1900 the DMA President, and John Wilson, General Secretary of the Miners' National Association from 1895.

Copeland Road School Football Team, 1947-48. The trophy is the Bishop Auckland Schools Football League Championship of that year. Back left: Jackie Laidlaw, Jim Wilson, Eric Meads, Colin Summerson, Kenneth Stones, Kenneth Copeland, Malcolm Butcher, Tom Corner. Front: Tommy Longstaff, Billy Bannister, George Watson, Les Woodward, Tot Laskey, Cresswell Lamb, David Douthwaite. They had only previously won that trophy once, in 1931-32.

The West Auckland Cup Final Team of 1961. Back left: George Siddle, Colin Summerson, Albert Mendum (captain), Brian Bowmaker, Jimmy Stafford, Donny Carter. Front: Ray Briggs, Billy Broomfield, Ernie Curtis, Stan Skelton, Allan Douglass.

Colin Summerson's Amateur Cup Medal. On one side is a footballer and FA logo. On the other the occasion, team and individual details.

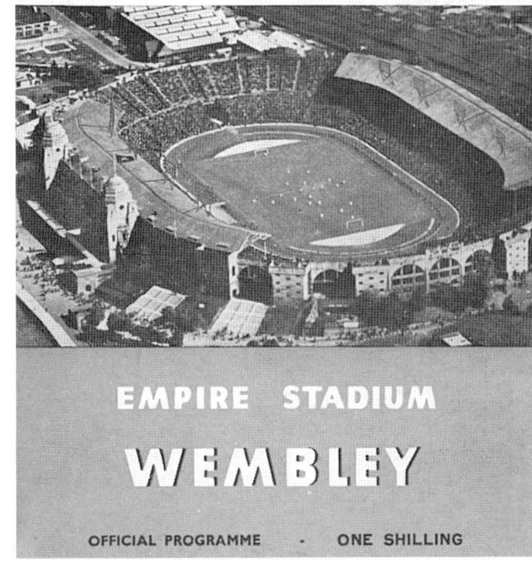

Programme from the 1961 FA Amateur Cup Final between West Auckland and Walthamstowe Avenue. West lost by 2-1, with Allan Douglass scoring.

St Helen's Junior School Football Team who won the local schools league championship and cup for three consecutive seasons. This picture is of their winning team in the third season, 1961-62. Left to right: Geoff Winter, Graham Meads, Jim Jackson, Dave Thomas (later Burnley, QPR, Everton, Wolves and England), Stuart Neesam, Tony Mundell, Michael Mills, Glen Dobinson, Malcolm Redford, David Jackson, Gareth Hall, Laurie Hammond.

Copeland Road Primary School, Class 2, 1997. Back left: Georgia Smallwood, Craig Hudson, Nathan Foster, Victoria Wallace, Jonathan Wade, Lucy I'Anson, Natasha Jacobs, Natalie Bell. Third row: Natasha Davies, Gareth Sanders, Christopher Morrell, Victoria Stoker, Adele Thompson, Kathryn Horsman, Steven Corner, Colin Williamson, Andrew Gates, Christopher Burke, Lauren Taylor. Second row: Joanne Swainston, Ashleigh Collinson, Mrs Jude, Lee Bryan, Sam Wilson, Sarah Goodfellow, Emma Curl. Front: James Turner, Sean Ebdon, Rachel Lyons, Jessica Lowry, Liam Danby, Sebastian Lamey, Kristopher Wooley, James Armstrong, Anita Winter, Daniel ?

Railways, Mining & Commerce

Cockfield station in North Eastern Railway days about 95 years ago; looking towards Bishop Auckland, with the road over the railway going down to The Slack. Cockfield itself is one mile along that road to the right. The station was about 650 feet above sea level. Stephen Elcoat was the stationmaster in those days.

In 1830 the Haggerleases branch of the Stockton & Darlington Railway (S&D) was completed along the Gaunless Valley from West Auckland to a terminus called Butterknowle goods station at Low Wham. Extensions to the branch were built by various coal owners as it was evident that the railway was an efficient, cheap means of moving coal. This branch lasted until 30th September 1963. The other railway line, promoted by the S&D, was the Bishop Auckland – Barnard Castle branch of the South Durham & Lancashire Union Railway which left the Haggerleases branch west of Spring Gardens, West Auckland and climbed along the valley side through Ramshaw and Cockfield to a summit at Gibsneese before descending into Langleydale and Barnard Castle. This line was part of the traffic of coke from County Durham to Cumberland and iron-ore from Cumberland to steelworks at Spennymoor and Teesside.

There was a passenger service on this line until 1962, which had previously brought about the closure of a limited passenger service on the Haggerleases branch in 1872. Coal mining was commercially important for about 120 years from 1840. Many early pits were family concerns where farming and mining went hand-in-hand. Coal was comparatively easy to dig from the shallow seams and the coming of the railways made it easy to market that coal. A list of mines in 1896 showed 25 mines employing 3125 men, and pits ranged in size from eight men at Copley to 449 at Randolph.

The economic slump after the First World War led to loss of markets and unemployment. Many collieries were flooded as water from the Gaunless and tributaries flowed into shallow workings, so that by 1936 a huge underground reservoir extended from Evenwood towards Bishop Auckland. Efficient pumping out of that water did not occur until 1947 when the National Coal Board was set up. However, many of the Gaunless Valley mines were worked out by then, and only 1073 men employed at 16 mines, half at Randolph/Gordon House Collieries. Deep mining closed at Randolph in 1960 (Hutton Drift in 1962) and drift mining at West Auckland in 1967. Since then some opencast mining, particularly north of the Gaunless, has continued. Small private mines at Low Lands had all closed by 1968.

Another view of Cockfield station in the 1950s, with a train from Bishop Auckland probably to Middleton-in-Teesdale, pulled by class A8, No 69875 locomotive of West Auckland shed. This station closed to passengers in 1958.

Lands or Gaunless Viaduct, with a train crossing it heading for the next station at Cockfield. Underneath is the Haggerleases branch. Lands Viaduct was 640 feet long and 93 feet above the River Gaunless. The viaduct was widened from single to double track in 1903.

This siding at Low Lands is on the Haggerleases branch. At the top left just visible is a bridge over the Bishop Auckland – Barnard Castle line. The screens of Gordon House Colliery are visible behind the chimney.

Two views of Evenwood station – which was actually in Ramshaw on the other side of the Gaunless. The top view looking towards Cockfield shows the station as originally built in 1863 with a single track. It was doubled later as can be seen on the lower picture which shows a train from Bishop Auckland arriving. Note the new wooden platform and shelter on the left. The lower postcard was sent from M. Clarke, 6 Raby Moor, Cockfield on 19th February 1906 to a Mrs G. Pollit, 56 Cold Bath Road, Harrogate. He refers to adding this card to her collection. In 1906 the stationmaster at Evenwood was George H. Coates. The station closed to passengers in 1957.

Spring Gardens in 1895 where the A68 road crossed the railway about half-a-mile north west of West Auckland village centre. The building to the left is the Earl Grey Inn. Behind the camera the 1830 Haggerleases branch railway and the newer 1862 line to Barnard Castle diverge, the former running along the bottom of the Gaunless Valley and the latter line climbing above the river valley in order to cross into the valley of the River Tees just beyond Cockfield Fell.

West Auckland station level crossing over the A688 road on 3rd March 1962. In the background is West Auckland Colliery. The signalman is T. Lee.

West Auckland station in the late 1950s. Railway passenger services had originally started in 1833 when a coach service operated from St Helen's to Shildon by a Mr Graham, and in 1834 when a Mr West started a service from St Helen's to Lands crossing. Only in 1856 when a service from Bishop Auckland to St Helen's via Shildon Tunnel Junction commenced, were steam locomotives used.

West Auckland station showing clearly the unusual platform layout. The overbridge had been demolished by 1962 when the station closed.

A view from the carriage window of the 4.15 pm train from Bishop Auckland to Barnard Castle as it nears West Auckland on a snowy 27th February 1962, just four months before the line closed.

West Auckland station on the same date as the previous picture, as the train leaves for Barnard Castle. Note the two platforms – not facing each other as normal. The train crew and station staff posing for the photographer, Ian S. Carr.

Locomotive 'Carbon' working on the Haggerleases branch at the Butterknowle end in the 1920s. E.M. Widdas was the driver.

North Eastern Railway J27 class locomotive bringing empties to Low Lands for Gordon House Colliery via the Haggerleases branch in about 1920.

The Drift, Cockfield Fell. The Gaunless Valley was characterised by many small pits, some of them employing only a few men, and some of them here today and gone tomorrow. For instance in 1896 Copley employed only 8 men and Hummerbeck at West Auckland only 21. Hummerbeck actually closed only two years later after a life of less than 20 years.

Mostyn Colliery, Cockfield. Later known as Gordon House, the first colliery was sunk in the 1860/70s on Cockfield Fell, and worked by W.H. Hedley & Co based at Norwood, Ramshaw. In 1893 a new winning to the Brockwell seam was made, and by 1896 the pit employed 328 men. By then it was owned by the North Bitchburn Coal Co and managed by Thomas Snowdon.

Two more photographs of Gordon House taken in the late 1950s. Percy Widdas was the manager from at least 1906 to 1925 by which time the pit had been sited further south than the original. Gordon House employed 504 men in 1930 and 472 in 1940. In 1950 it merged with Randolph Colliery, Evenwood. The pit closed in 1961.

Randolph Colliery from the east. The colliery was sunk in 1893 by the North Bitchburn Coal Co to tap the Hutton, Harvey, Busty and Brockwell seams. Its first manager was Thomas Heslop and in the early days employed 450 men, which had increased to 824 in 1930 when Thomas H. Blaiklock was in charge. 221 men were employed in 1962 when the Hutton Drift mine closed. The deep mine had closed two years earlier.

An aerial view of Randolph Colliery. The waggonway running off the picture to the north connects with the Haggerleases branch about half-a-mile away in the Gaunless Valley. Randolph cokeworks were a famous landmark in South West Durham from 1895 until closed by Coalite Ltd in 1984, as was the conical pit-heap, Randolph South which was re-claimed in 1987.

Setting alight timber to demolish a chimney at Woodland Colliery. This photograph is dated as 1914, but there is some evidence that it could be later – such as the late 20s. This colliery once supplied enough coal to fire 196 coke ovens in the immediate area.

Coal washing plant at West Auckland Colliery in 1960. It seems ironic that washing plants and pithead baths were extensively installed in the 1950s, yet many pits did not stay open for very long after. This drift mine closed in 1967.

Private enterprise at Butterknowle. The upper picture is of a delivery cart outside Joseph Kellett's, grocers, provisions & drapers. Kellett's also ran the post office and appeared in Kelly's Directories in 1906 and 1925. The lower picture is of the butcher's cart on his daily delivery 100 years ago.

The Co-operative society was well represented in the Gaunless Valley with the Bishop Auckland Industrial Co-operative Flour & Provision Society having premises at Butterknowle, Evenwood and West Auckland at the time of the society's golden jubilee in 1910. Butterknowle branch was opened in 1885 when a house and shop were leased from a Mr Dowson at £30 per year. In 1890, having bought land fronting on to Pinfold Lane and Wham Lane, the society built its own shop which cost £2,500 including fittings and stables.

Evenwood branch opened in 1904 after a petition from local members. The building contract, which consisted of grocer's shop, warehouse, stables and manager's house, was let out for £1,273 13s 6d. I am not sure when West Auckland opened, but an estimate suggests between 1906-10.

The society made a new departure in 1898 when it took farms at Windlestone and Staindrop Field House, West Auckland. Neither farm was a success and both of them were given up in 1905, though Greenfield Farm at Etherley which had been taken on in 1900 was retained as a dairy farm. However, in the early years of the 20th century the Bishop Auckland Co-op Society, specifically in relation to the manager's and two other houses, belonging to the society in Butterknowle, became involved against the Butterknowle Coal Company regarding subsidence to their properties through coal mining. Four years of subsidence resulted in the society in 1902 asking the coal company for financial compensation or for repairs to the properties because of the coal company's underground workings under the houses. This case went to law, to the High Court, Court of Appeal, and finally the House of Lords in 1906. The Co-op won at every stage which established the principle that royalty owners and mine owners did not have the right to destroy or damage the surface. Co-op jubilation was short-lived in that the Butterknowle Coal Co could not pay legal costs of £2,500, and went into liquidation with the colliery closing and putting many Co-op members out of work. A firm of solicitors, Chipchase & Wood, took over the colliery and re-opened it in 1910 as New Butterknowle Colliery for about five years. Today, the only Co-operative shop in the Gaunless Valley is at Cockfield. A shop which opened in the 1920s, but has outlasted its older neighbours.

Butterknowle premises where the manager in 1910 was John Gent. James A. Parkin was the manager from 1885 to 1908 covering the period of subsidence and the court case. These premises closed in 1968.

Evenwood premises with house attached where John Metcalfe lived when he was manager there from 1904. The premises are still there today, but closed in 1984, though the house is occupied.

West Auckland premises. Mr J.R. Mansfield manager in 1910.

The damaged premises at Butterknowle, inside and out. The manager's house and two other houses belonging to the Co-op.

Many of the book's illustrations have been of the long distant past. Let's end on the adults of the future. West Auckland – Copeland Road Primary School, Class 2, 1999. Back left: Robert Maddison, Gareth Morley, Luke Bannister, Sam Russell, Ryan Burke. Middle: Sarah Green, Anna Brassell, Danniele Hunt, Adele Sherlock, Beth Albury, Rebecca Wade. Front: Chelsea Wade, Lauren Cooper, Amy Meads, Mrs Milnes, Amy Chambers, Laura Metcalf, Justine Hopps.